American values, one story at a time.

Christine O'hare

Clara Barton - The Angel of the Battlefield

Illustrations by Dan Burr

Text copyright © Heroes of Liberty Inc., 2022

Illustrations copyright Heroes of Liberty Inc., 2022

1216 Broadway, New York, NY 10001

Heroes of Liberty Inc.
1216 Broadway, New York, NY 10001

Find more heroes to read about on:
WWW.HEROESOFLIBERTY.COM

Clara Barton

THE ANGEL OF
THE BATTLEFIELD

Clara Barton

When the Civil War broke out, Clara Barton felt she couldn't just sit tight until it was all over. There was just too much suffering all around her. Of course, the wounded soldiers suffered most. So she set out to do whatever she could for them: she tended to their wounds, secured clothes and medical supplies for them, even read them books and wrote letters to their families for them.

When the war was over, Clara Barton came to see that more could be done in the future, if help was better organized. This is why she founded the American Red Cross.

Ever since it was established in 1881, the Red Cross has been devoted to helping people in the wake of wars, plagues, and natural disasters. If a hurricane hits, or if battles take place, if a pandemic infects people, or a flood washes over their homes and fields, you can count on the American Red Cross to be there.

Clara Barton was also its first president.

RED CROSS RELIEF TO FLOOD VICTIMS, 1883
OHIO RIVER

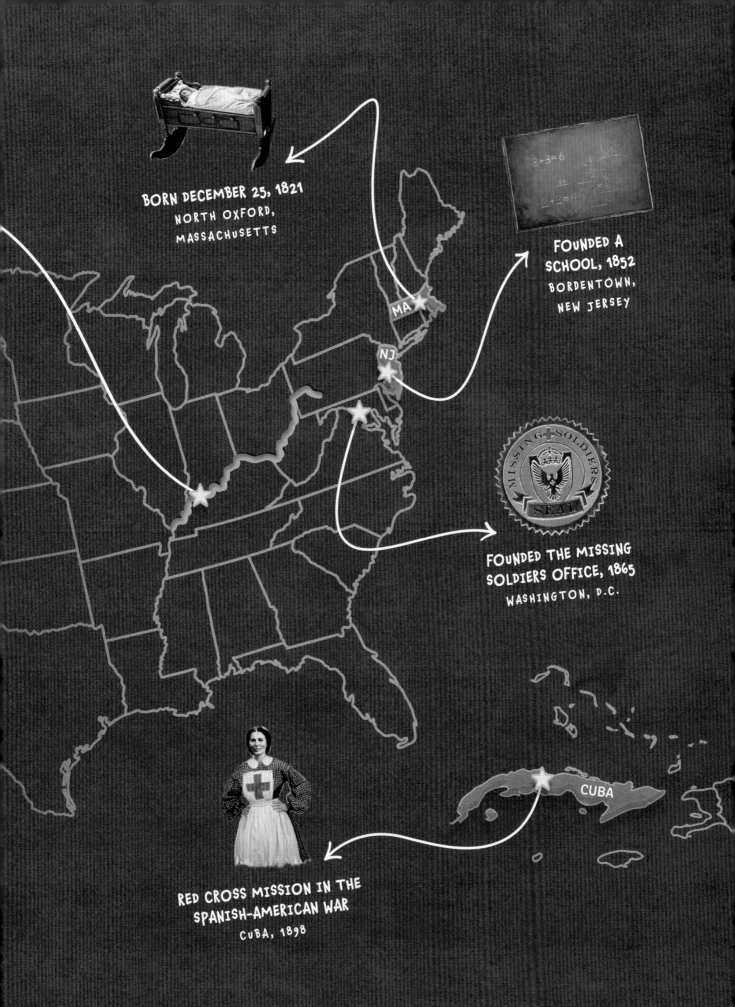

BORN DECEMBER 25, 1821
NORTH OXFORD,
MASSACHUSETTS

FOUNDED A
SCHOOL, 1852
BORDENTOWN,
NEW JERSEY

MA

NJ

FOUNDED THE MISSING
SOLDIERS OFFICE, 1865
WASHINGTON, D.C.

CUBA

RED CROSS MISSION IN THE
SPANISH-AMERICAN WAR
CUBA, 1898

It wasn't long after it was founded that the American Red Cross saw the first opportunity to prove how useful it could be. In 1883, the Ohio River swelled with water, and rose and flooded vast areas along its banks. Homes were washed away, farm animals were lost, crops were devastated, and debris was everywhere, floating in the water or just sitting in the mud. Families huddled together in wet clothes, with nowhere to go and no dry wood or coal to light fires with.

They were all in danger of freezing and of starving.

There was no way to reach these people by land because all the roads were overwhelmed by the flood. The Red Cross rented a big riverboat and dispatched help from the river to the banks: food, blankets, clothes, dry coal, and the material and tools for rebuilding houses. They even hired and brought carpenters to help do the job.

Ordinary people wanted to help too. Among them was a group of six children: Joe, Florence, Mary, Bertie, Loyd, and Reed. They wrote and performed a little show of song and dance, and they collected some money from their audiences. They managed to raise $51.25.

Clara Barton received their money along with a message that said the money should be used "where it would do the most good." They called themselves The Little Six.

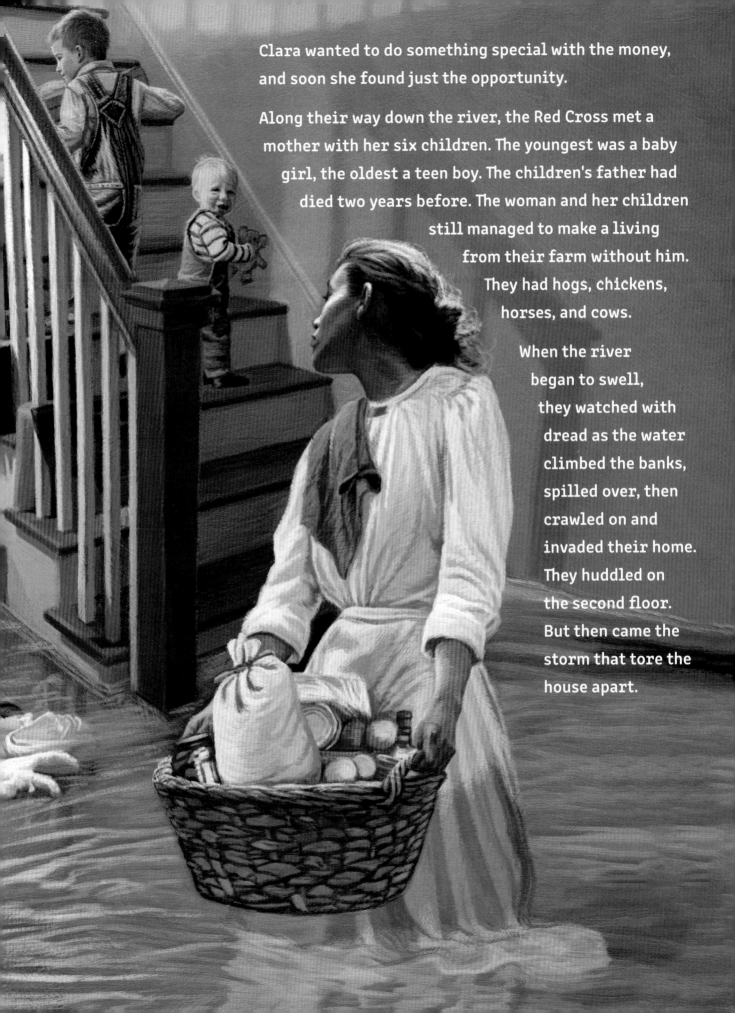

Clara wanted to do something special with the money, and soon she found just the opportunity.

Along their way down the river, the Red Cross met a mother with her six children. The youngest was a baby girl, the oldest a teen boy. The children's father had died two years before. The woman and her children still managed to make a living from their farm without him. They had hogs, chickens, horses, and cows.

When the river began to swell, they watched with dread as the water climbed the banks, spilled over, then crawled on and invaded their home. They huddled on the second floor. But then came the storm that tore the house apart.

When it was all over, the six children looked on at the ruins and silently wept. Who can ever know the despair of a mother's heart, when her tired hands can offer so little to her babies?

But life goes on, and you can't just give up. The mother got to work setting up a shelter in a storage shed, together with the chickens that survived. She saved what food she could salvage and kept the place as tidy as she could to make it feel a little more like home.

When the Red Cross boat arrived, it brought with it a ray of hope. Seeing that the farm was in ruins, Clara Barton asked the woman if she would want to leave and maybe go back to where she grew up.

The woman said she didn't. "My husband is buried here," she said. "I will not leave him alone. Besides, my six children can visit his grave, and it gives them some comfort."

Suddenly, Clara knew what she would do. Six children! That rang a bell. And so she offered the woman the money that The Little Six had raised with their show. "Would that money help?" she asked.

After a silence, her voice choked with tears, the woman finally said: "God knows how much it would be to me. With my good children's help, we can build a home again."

The Red Cross supplemented the sum to total $100. That was a lot of money back then. And just before they left, the woman said she had a name for the new home. She would call it, she said, The Little Six.

Clara Barton was born Clarissa Harlowe Barton in North Oxford, Massachusetts, on December 25, 1821. Her family was well off. Her father was a successful businessman and a captain in the militia, and he fought in the Ohio Indian Wars. He captivated his daughter's imagination with his war stories. And ever since, she admired the brave men who were ready to risk life and limb to protect their families, their people, and their nation. In the future, she would devote much of her time to helping them.

As a child, Clara was a good student. But she was painfully shy. She kept to herself most of the time, and she rarely spoke in class. And she made few friends.

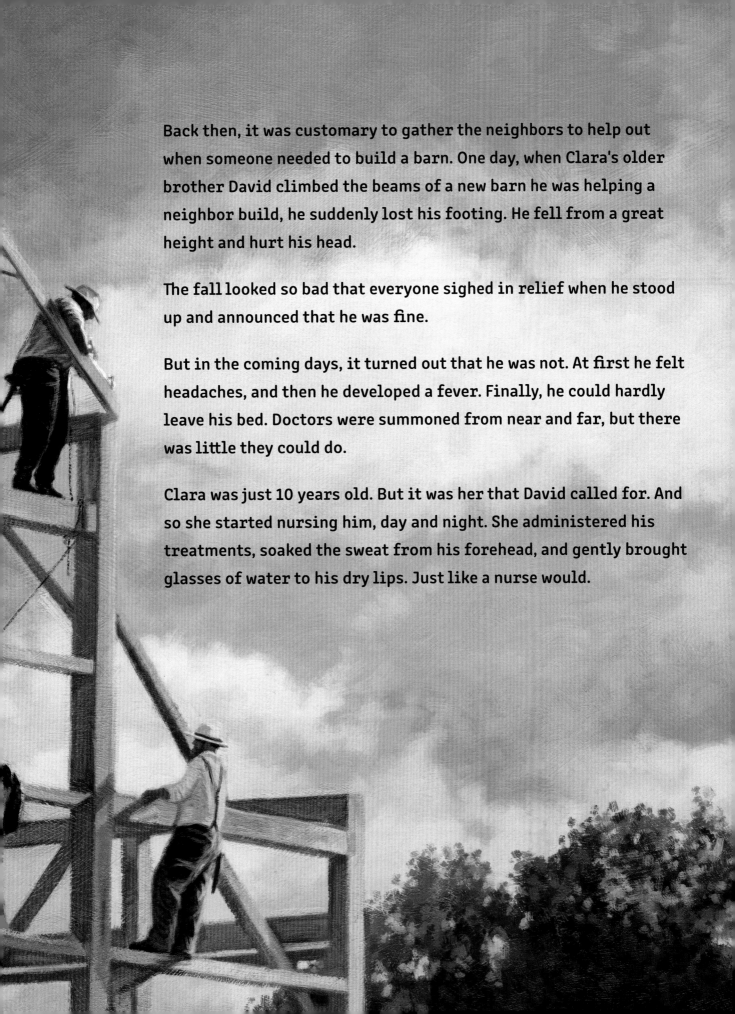

Back then, it was customary to gather the neighbors to help out when someone needed to build a barn. One day, when Clara's older brother David climbed the beams of a new barn he was helping a neighbor build, he suddenly lost his footing. He fell from a great height and hurt his head.

The fall looked so bad that everyone sighed in relief when he stood up and announced that he was fine.

But in the coming days, it turned out that he was not. At first he felt headaches, and then he developed a fever. Finally, he could hardly leave his bed. Doctors were summoned from near and far, but there was little they could do.

Clara was just 10 years old. But it was her that David called for. And so she started nursing him, day and night. She administered his treatments, soaked the sweat from his forehead, and gently brought glasses of water to his dry lips. Just like a nurse would.

After a while, doctors gave up on David. They thought he would never be back on his feet. Seasons came and seasons went, and he was not getting any better.

But little Clara would not give up. For two years she barely left the house and persisted in her nursing until finally David began to improve. In time, he recovered completely and once again became the strong young man that he was before his injury. David was grateful to his little sister, not just for her care, but for refusing to give up on him when others did.

David was the first of many, many patients Clara would go on to help.

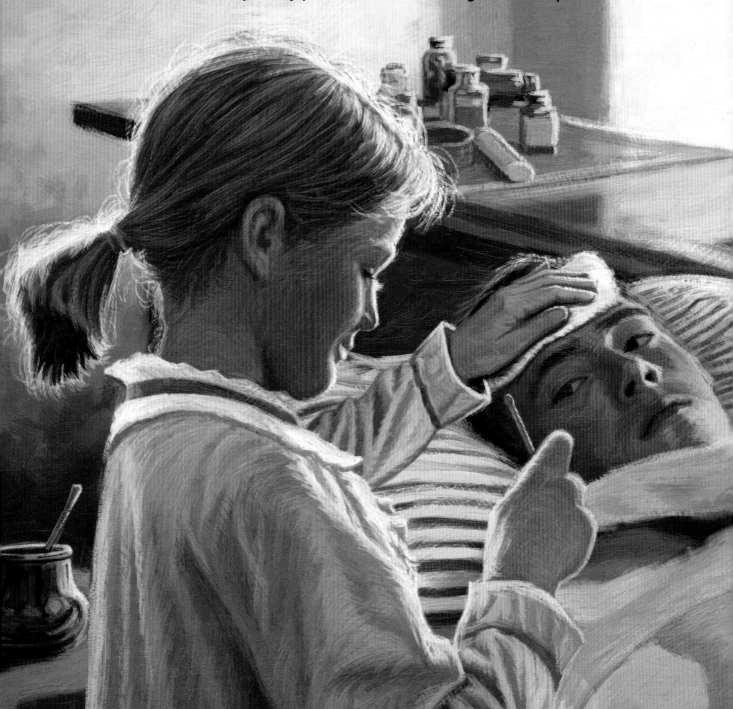

When Clara grew a little older, her parents hoped that sending her to a high school away from home would help cure her shyness. But they were wrong. Away from her family, with children who were complete strangers, she seemed to retreat further into herself.

Once, when she summoned the courage to speak in class, it ended in tears. She had studied hard, and when another child could not remember the name of an ancient Egyptian king, she jumped in and said "Potlomy."

The other children burst out laughing. This is not how you pronounce the name 'Ptolemy'. The 'p' is silent and the 'o' belongs after the 't.' As the teacher explained, it should sound like this: To-le-mi. But Clara was no longer listening. The laughter of the class was still ringing in her ears. It felt like a slap on her face. She couldn't stop her tears.

The longer she stayed in school, the more reserved she became. She lost her appetite and eventually got sick. Her parents took her back home. They worried that their daughter would never become independent enough to take care of herself.

Little did they know! Who could have guessed this shy child would become a real trailblazer?

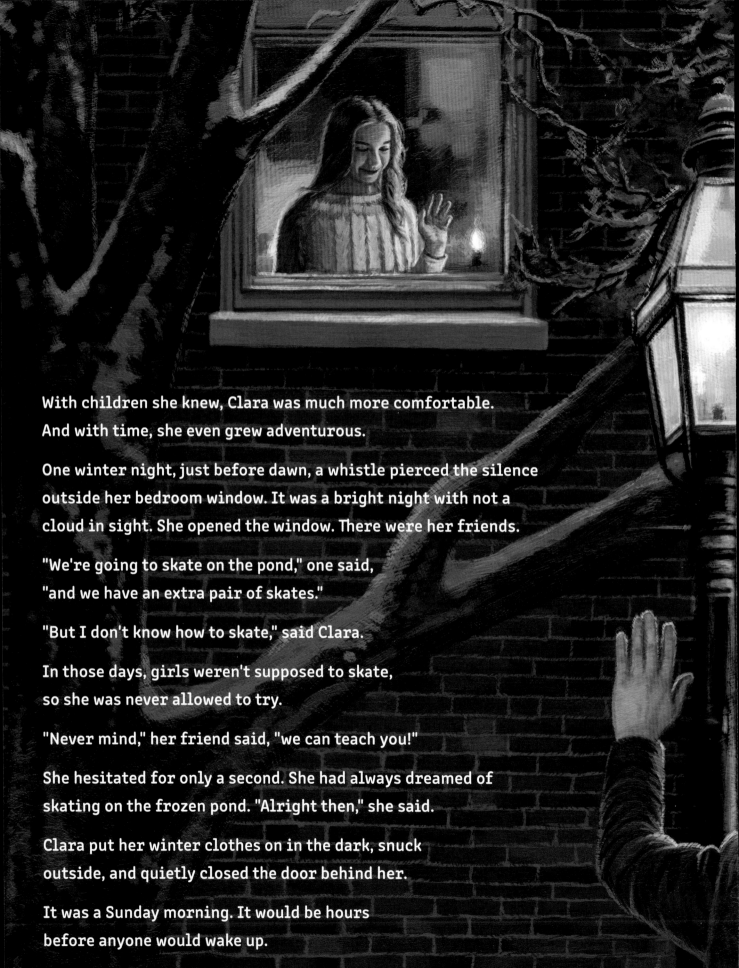

With children she knew, Clara was much more comfortable.
And with time, she even grew adventurous.

One winter night, just before dawn, a whistle pierced the silence
outside her bedroom window. It was a bright night with not a
cloud in sight. She opened the window. There were her friends.

"We're going to skate on the pond," one said,
"and we have an extra pair of skates."

"But I don't know how to skate," said Clara.

In those days, girls weren't supposed to skate,
so she was never allowed to try.

"Never mind," her friend said, "we can teach you!"

She hesitated for only a second. She had always dreamed of
skating on the frozen pond. "Alright then," she said.

Clara put her winter clothes on in the dark, snuck
outside, and quietly closed the door behind her.

It was a Sunday morning. It would be hours
before anyone would wake up.

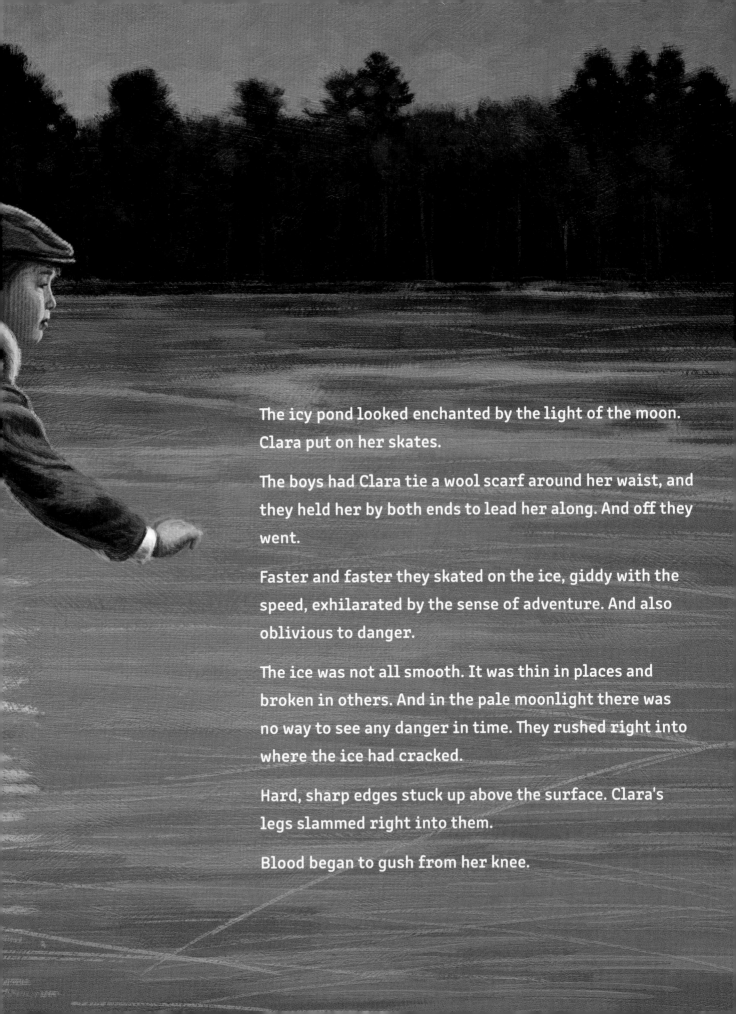

The icy pond looked enchanted by the light of the moon. Clara put on her skates.

The boys had Clara tie a wool scarf around her waist, and they held her by both ends to lead her along. And off they went.

Faster and faster they skated on the ice, giddy with the speed, exhilarated by the sense of adventure. And also oblivious to danger.

The ice was not all smooth. It was thin in places and broken in others. And in the pale moonlight there was no way to see any danger in time. They rushed right into where the ice had cracked.

Hard, sharp edges stuck up above the surface. Clara's legs slammed right into them.

Blood began to gush from her knee.

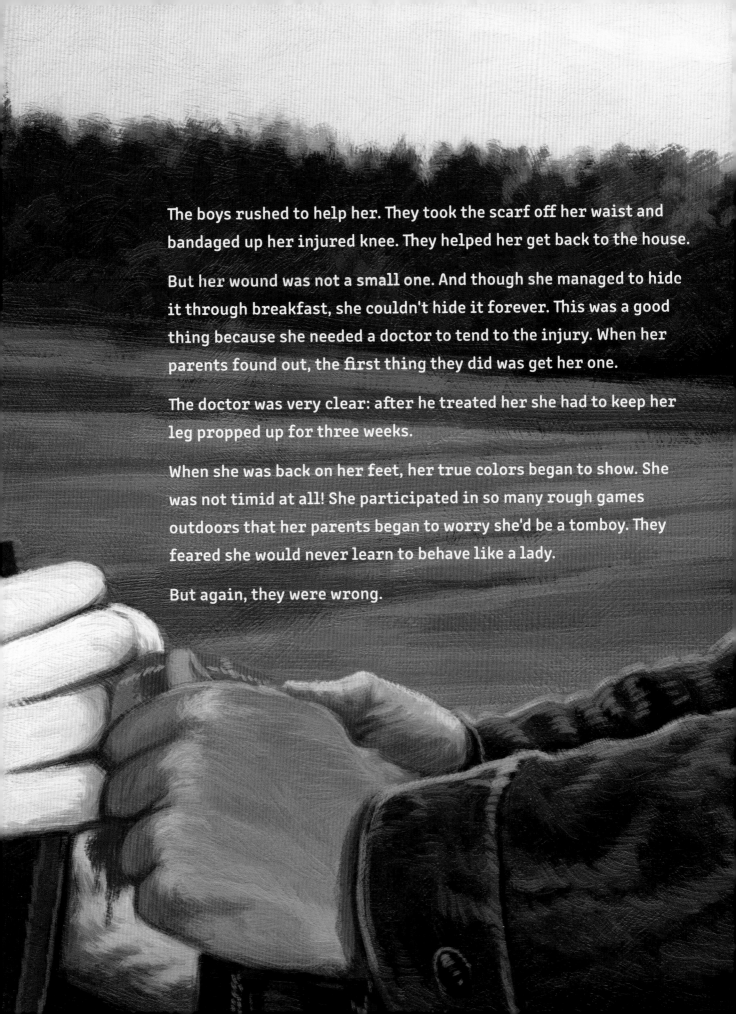

The boys rushed to help her. They took the scarf off her waist and bandaged up her injured knee. They helped her get back to the house.

But her wound was not a small one. And though she managed to hide it through breakfast, she couldn't hide it forever. This was a good thing because she needed a doctor to tend to the injury. When her parents found out, the first thing they did was get her one.

The doctor was very clear: after he treated her she had to keep her leg propped up for three weeks.

When she was back on her feet, her true colors began to show. She was not timid at all! She participated in so many rough games outdoors that her parents began to worry she'd be a tomboy. They feared she would never learn to behave like a lady.

But again, they were wrong.

Her outdoor games taught her valuable lessons. When she decided to become a teacher, they served her well. She knew how to handle even the most noisy, rowdy boys in her class. And she was able to do it without raising her voice. She understood the children and they respected her authority.

Once, when she saw the boys playing outside recklessly and putting themselves in danger, she decided to step into the game and teach them by example.

The lads, she would write later, "soon perceived that I was no stranger to their sports or their tricks; that my early education had not been neglected, and that they were not the first boys I had seen. When they found that I was as agile and as strong as themselves, that my throw was as sure and as straight as theirs, and that if they won a game it was because I permitted it, their respect knew no bounds."

When the school year ended and she parted with her class, some of the kids were in tears.

Having gained experience in teaching, Clara decided to found her own school in Bordentown, New Jersey. She ran it well, and it was a great success. But eventually the school board elected a man to run it. In those days, many believed that it was not for women to run big institutions.

It would not be long before Clara would show them they were wrong. She would go on to run a much bigger organization, and once again it would be one she would create herself.

But in the meantime, great events were upon the United States. In 1860, Abraham Lincoln was elected president. The Southern states where slavery was legal understood what his election meant: the days of slavery were numbered within the United States. And so they decided to break away and create their own separate nation. They called it the Confederate States of America.

Lincoln would have none of it. We are one nation, he declared, and all should respect the will of the majority that elected him to the presidency. He called the Confederates "rebels" and vowed to impose the authority of the laws of the United States on them, by force, if need be.

It soon turned out that a great deal of force would be needed. More Americans were killed in the Civil War than in all other wars the nation has fought combined.

When the first wounded soldiers began to arrive in Washington, D.C., where Clara lived back then, she headed to the train station at once. She had heard so much from her father about soldiers and the sacrifices they made, and she wanted to help them in any way she could.

What she found at the station was beyond words. Men in torn uniforms were hungry, wounded, and desperate. She set out at once to provide them with first aid.

After the wounded were housed in the unfinished Capitol Building, she went about arranging for aid and supplies to be brought there.

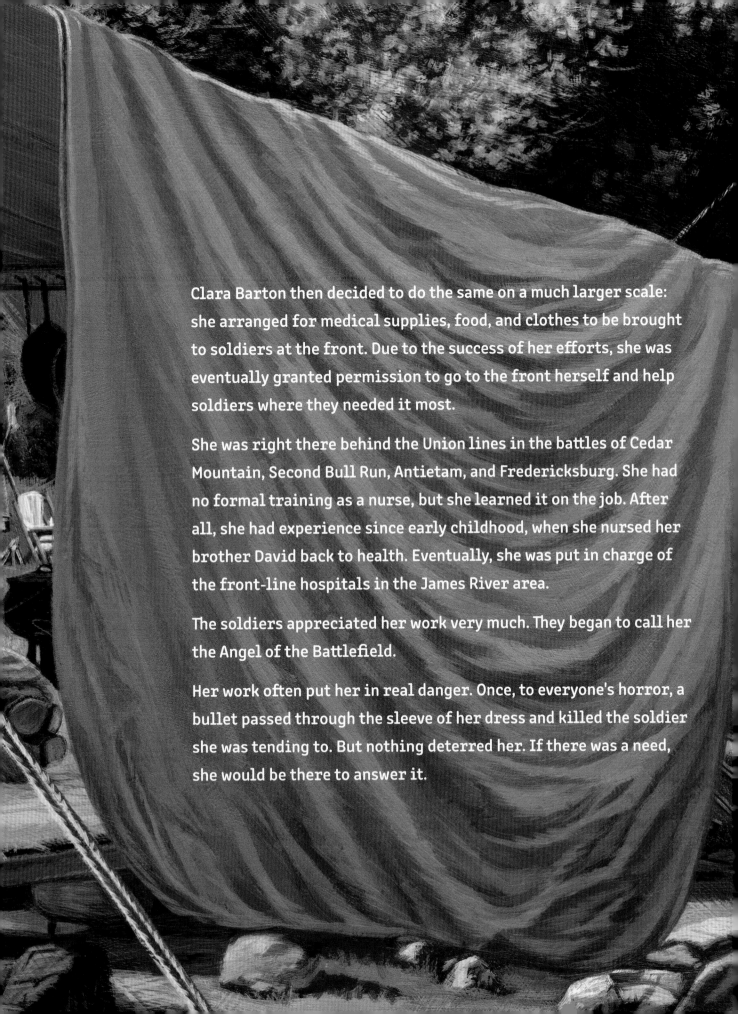

Clara Barton then decided to do the same on a much larger scale: she arranged for medical supplies, food, and clothes to be brought to soldiers at the front. Due to the success of her efforts, she was eventually granted permission to go to the front herself and help soldiers where they needed it most.

She was right there behind the Union lines in the battles of Cedar Mountain, Second Bull Run, Antietam, and Fredericksburg. She had no formal training as a nurse, but she learned it on the job. After all, she had experience since early childhood, when she nursed her brother David back to health. Eventually, she was put in charge of the front-line hospitals in the James River area.

The soldiers appreciated her work very much. They began to call her the Angel of the Battlefield.

Her work often put her in real danger. Once, to everyone's horror, a bullet passed through the sleeve of her dress and killed the soldier she was tending to. But nothing deterred her. If there was a need, she would be there to answer it.

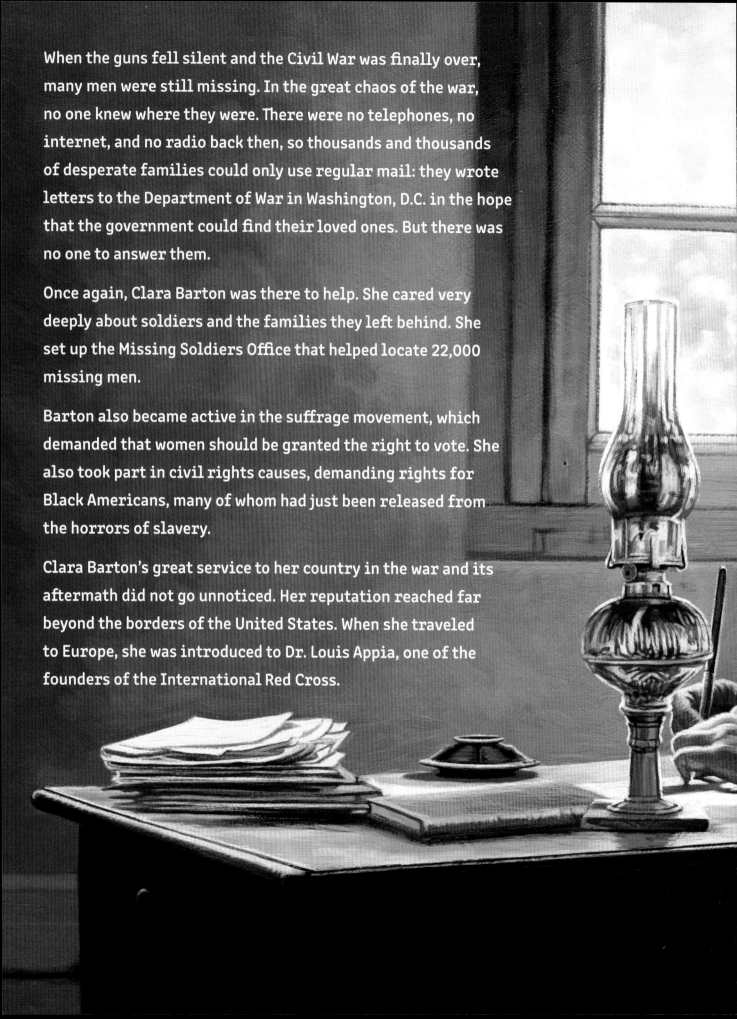

When the guns fell silent and the Civil War was finally over, many men were still missing. In the great chaos of the war, no one knew where they were. There were no telephones, no internet, and no radio back then, so thousands and thousands of desperate families could only use regular mail: they wrote letters to the Department of War in Washington, D.C. in the hope that the government could find their loved ones. But there was no one to answer them.

Once again, Clara Barton was there to help. She cared very deeply about soldiers and the families they left behind. She set up the Missing Soldiers Office that helped locate 22,000 missing men.

Barton also became active in the suffrage movement, which demanded that women should be granted the right to vote. She also took part in civil rights causes, demanding rights for Black Americans, many of whom had just been released from the horrors of slavery.

Clara Barton's great service to her country in the war and its aftermath did not go unnoticed. Her reputation reached far beyond the borders of the United States. When she traveled to Europe, she was introduced to Dr. Louis Appia, one of the founders of the International Red Cross.

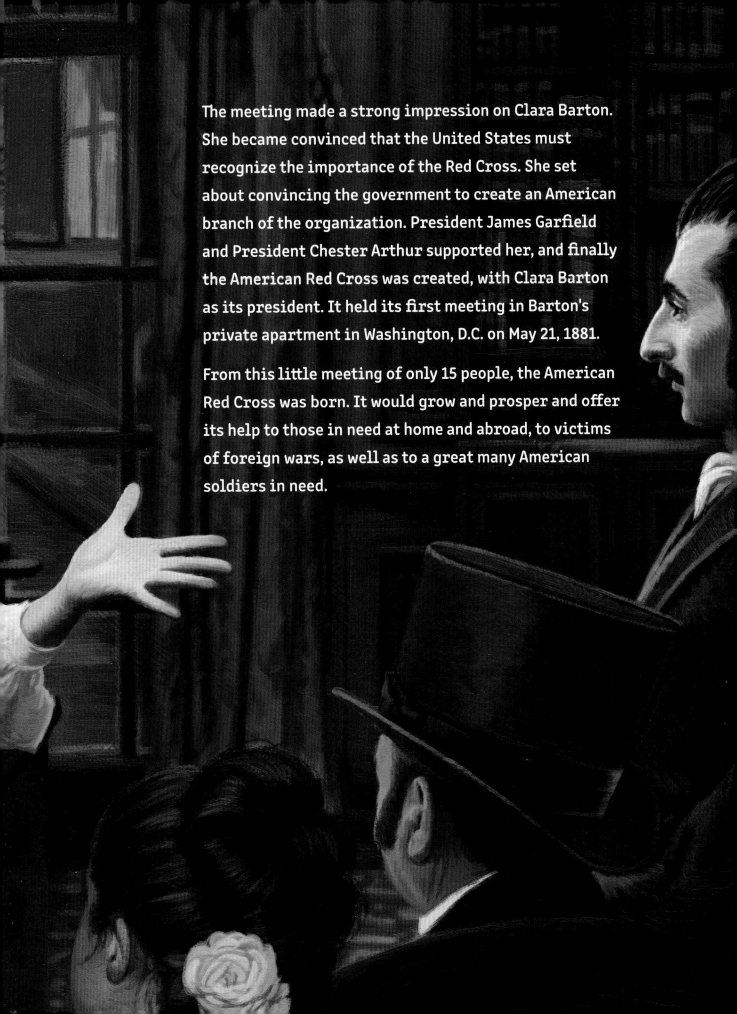

The meeting made a strong impression on Clara Barton. She became convinced that the United States must recognize the importance of the Red Cross. She set about convincing the government to create an American branch of the organization. President James Garfield and President Chester Arthur supported her, and finally the American Red Cross was created, with Clara Barton as its president. It held its first meeting in Barton's private apartment in Washington, D.C. on May 21, 1881.

From this little meeting of only 15 people, the American Red Cross was born. It would grow and prosper and offer its help to those in need at home and abroad, to victims of foreign wars, as well as to a great many American soldiers in need.

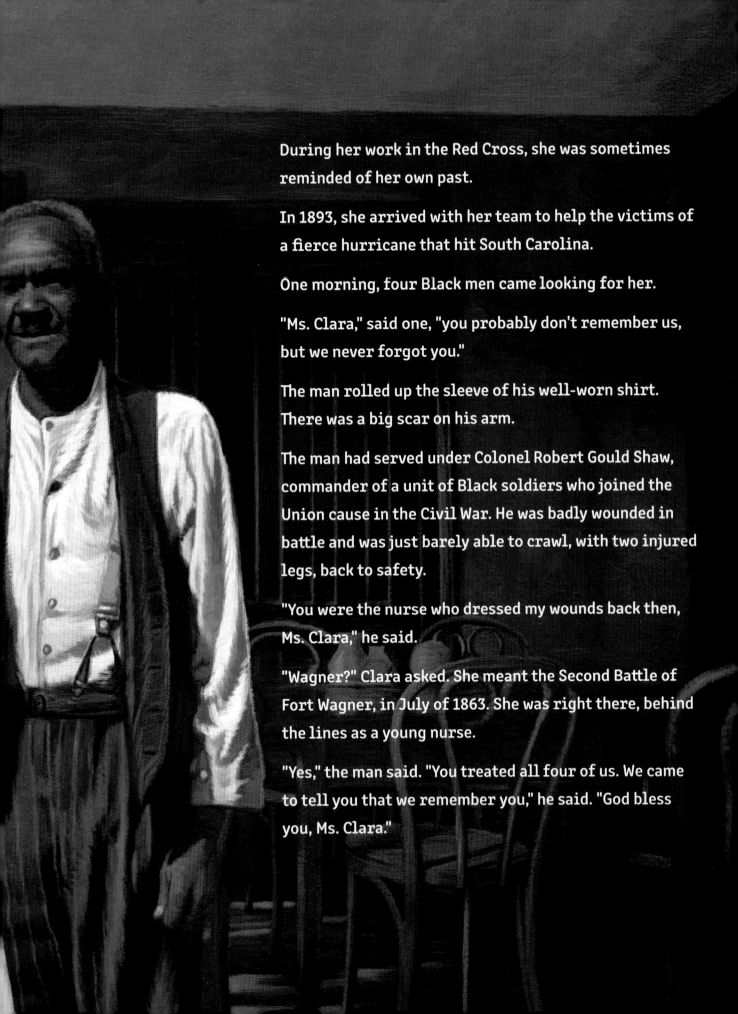

During her work in the Red Cross, she was sometimes reminded of her own past.

In 1893, she arrived with her team to help the victims of a fierce hurricane that hit South Carolina.

One morning, four Black men came looking for her.

"Ms. Clara," said one, "you probably don't remember us, but we never forgot you."

The man rolled up the sleeve of his well-worn shirt. There was a big scar on his arm.

The man had served under Colonel Robert Gould Shaw, commander of a unit of Black soldiers who joined the Union cause in the Civil War. He was badly wounded in battle and was just barely able to crawl, with two injured legs, back to safety.

"You were the nurse who dressed my wounds back then, Ms. Clara," he said.

"Wagner?" Clara asked. She meant the Second Battle of Fort Wagner, in July of 1863. She was right there, behind the lines as a young nurse.

"Yes," the man said. "You treated all four of us. We came to tell you that we remember you," he said. "God bless you, Ms. Clara."

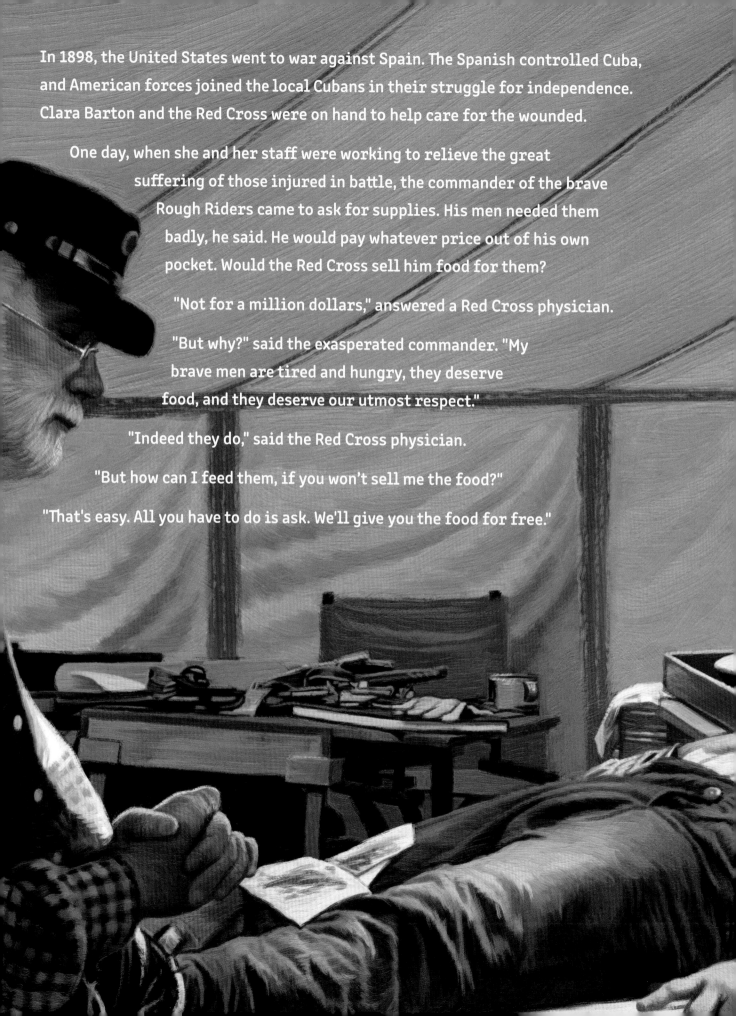

In 1898, the United States went to war against Spain. The Spanish controlled Cuba, and American forces joined the local Cubans in their struggle for independence. Clara Barton and the Red Cross were on hand to help care for the wounded.

One day, when she and her staff were working to relieve the great suffering of those injured in battle, the commander of the brave Rough Riders came to ask for supplies. His men needed them badly, he said. He would pay whatever price out of his own pocket. Would the Red Cross sell him food for them?

"Not for a million dollars," answered a Red Cross physician.

"But why?" said the exasperated commander. "My brave men are tired and hungry, they deserve food, and they deserve our utmost respect."

"Indeed they do," said the Red Cross physician.

"But how can I feed them, if you won't sell me the food?"

"That's easy. All you have to do is ask. We'll give you the food for free."

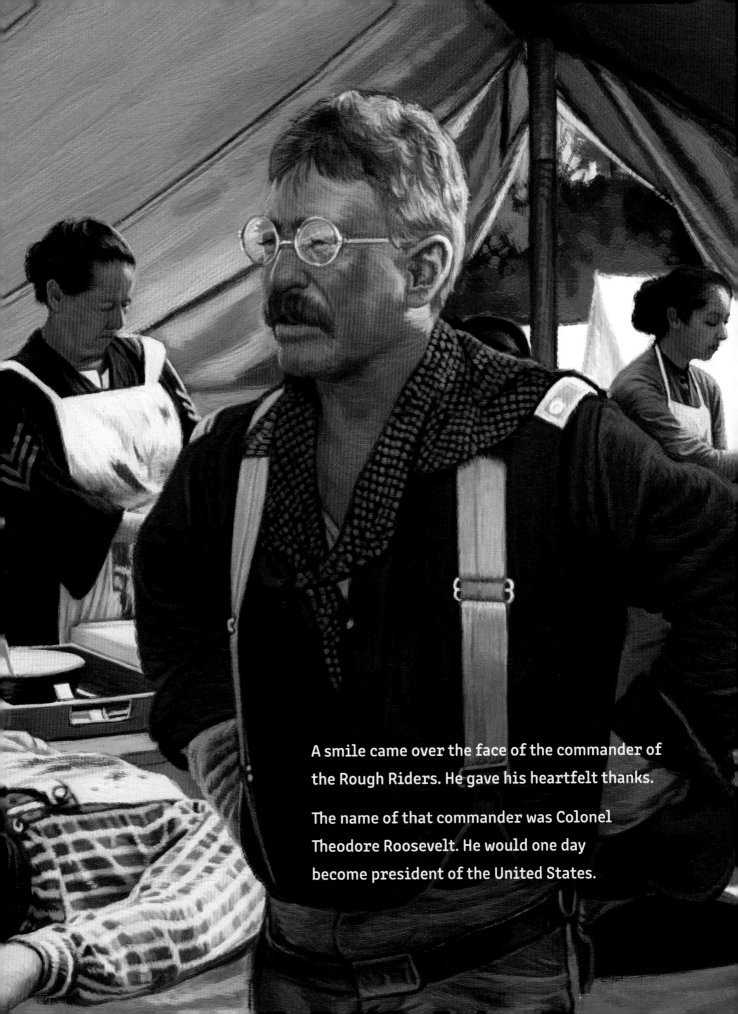

A smile came over the face of the commander of the Rough Riders. He gave his heartfelt thanks.

The name of that commander was Colonel Theodore Roosevelt. He would one day become president of the United States.

By the time Clara Barton reached old age, she had become famous. School children wrote her many letters asking not just about her work, but also about her life, and especially what she was like as a child. Clara Barton never married and never had children of her own. Nevertheless, she loved the nation's children, and felt she had responsibility toward them all. And so she set out to write the story of her own childhood in a little book. She dedicated it to all school children, and this is what she wrote on its first page:

Dear Children of the Schools:

Your oft-repeated appeals have reached me. They are too many and too earnest to be disregarded; and because of them, and because of my love for you, I have dedicated this little book to you. I have made it small, that you may the more easily read it. I have done it in the hope that it may give you pleasure, and in the wish that, when you shall be women and men, you may each remember, as I do, that you were once a child, full of childish thoughts and action, but of whom it was said, "Suffer them to come unto Me, and forbid them not, for of such is the Kingdom of Heaven."

Faithfully your friend,

CLARA BARTON

Like many American children before you, now you too have read about Clara Barton's life and work. When you are a little older, perhaps you would want to read her book *The Story of My Childhood*. And you will maybe then see that great heroes were once children too, just like you. And they too had more than just childish thoughts. They had big dreams. And this great country of ours, the United States of America, is where big dreams can actually come true. It is here that each and every one of you can someday achieve great things, as Clara Barton did. After all, every one of her great achievements started with dreams, just like yours.

7

INTERESTING FACTS ABOUT

Clara Barton

CLARA BARTON WAS INDUCTED INTO THE
NATIONAL WOMEN'S HALL OF FAME IN 1973.

SHE WAS BORN ON
CHRISTMAS DAY.

SHE WAS NAMED AFTER THE PROTAGONIST OF
SAMUEL RICHARDSON'S NOVEL 'CLARISSA'.

FROM CHILDHOOD, CLARA LOVED TO RIDE HORSES AND WAS ALWAYS COMFORTABLE IN THE SADDLE.

WHEN SHE SOUGHT ABRAHAM LINCOLN'S AGREEMENT TO OPENING THE MISSING SOLDIERS OFFICE, SHE WROTE A LETTER IN LARGE AND VERY FANCY HANDWRITING, SO IT WOULD STAND OUT AMONG HIS CORRESPONDENCE.

AFTER A HURRICANE DEVASTATED HUGE CROPS OF STRAWBERRIES IN TEXAS, SHE ARRANGED FOR THE DONATION OF 1.5 MILLION STRAWBERRY PLANTS TO TEXAS FARMERS.

SHE LOVED CHILDREN BUT WAS NEVER MARRIED AND HAD NONE OF HER OWN.